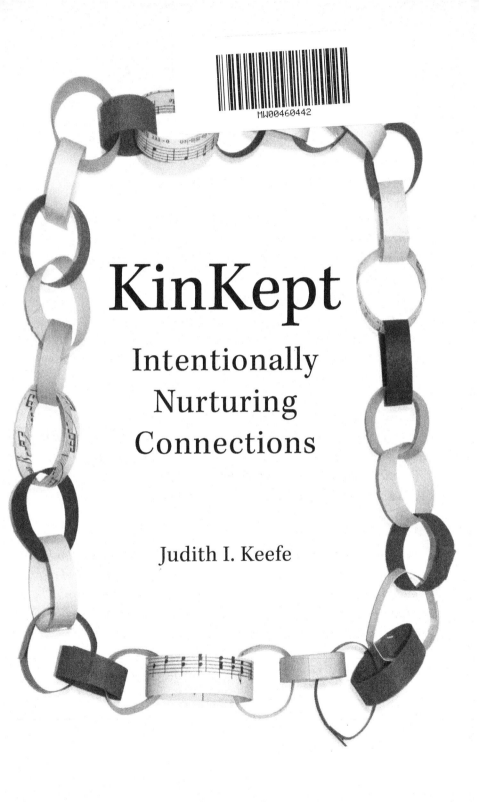

KinKept

Intentionally Nurturing Connections

Judith I. Keefe

*"I have never met Judy Keefe in person. In fact, our work together was done, largely, via email. However, from the moment she agreed to help me re-establish myself as a physician in the medical world, I felt cared for. I did not have the word at the time, but now I know that I felt **KinKept**.*

I adored this book from the moment I saw the paperchains that adorn its cover and its pages. During my recent work in a group setting, we used paperchains as a way to create community and then to decorate the room with thoughts and feelings, written on the links, from each person in the group. Everyone had the opportunity to see her or his own contribution to the whole, a wonderful metaphor reflected in Keefe's work, 'As we chose our colors, cut and pasted, and cooperated in connecting the loops, each one of us was important in the project.'

Written on the pages of this book, Judy Keefe includes, ' ... stories [that] relate times when others helped me feel like I belonged, and like I MATTERED.' By reading these lovely vignettes, we are reminded of the times that others helped us to feel like we belonged and like we mattered and - perhaps, the times we did the same for those we care about.

Ms. Keefe includes many thoughtful aspects of KinKeeping. None was more important or timely for me as I re-enter the world of medicine than was her essay in which she writes, 'I have to be my own best friend. I have to be my own cheerleader. No one else could possibly KNOW what it's like to be me.' "

—Jill Becker, MD., MA.

"Judith I. Keefe's delightfully gentle book, **KinKept: Intentionally Nurturing Connections,** *insightfully speaks of true engagement, of being together, cooperating, laughing, hugging, and achieving intimacy—keeping our kin!*

Our digital world lacks connection, oddly enough—that is, real connection. We passively respond to posts rather than physically engage our friends and loved ones—we don't touch each other anymore. We create selfies for our Facebook pages, hoping others will "like" us. We sit at tables together at restaurants, checking our smart phones, while ignoring those who sit beside us. We fail to recognize that in our frenzied search for online approval we are losing the very connections that could bring us joy, the very community we seek.

Perusing Judy's delightful examples of KinKeeping, the reader is challenged to develop his or her own KinKeeping. Examples in her book include making room for each other (and for all creatures), forgiving, affirming, making allowances, giving mercy, interjecting kindness, and playfulness; coming together in times of stress, hardship, happiness and celebration; in other words, what Judy calls, 'opening our hearts to one another.'

KinKept *challenges us to remember what makes us human and what is the best part of our humanity. Like the links of Judy's childhood paperchain, we are bound together through KinKeeping and we are restored to the community we crave. This little jewel of a book, if applied, promises to restore what we may not realize we have lost."*

—Linda Miner, Ph.D.

KinKept

Intentionally Nurturing Connections

Judith I. Keefe

ISBN: 978-0-9973857-0-0

KinKept—Intentionally Nurturing Connections, © 2017
by Judith I. Keefe
Published by KinKeeping Matters
Tulsa, OK

Printed in the United States of America

This work is dedicated to my own closest Kin, of all three kinds: kin by blood connection, kin by law connection, and kin by choice. I've been well and truly KinKept by these KinGroups, and I'm forever grateful.

I've learned so much from each of you dear KinKeepers, especially my children and their families. Thank you for always loving, teaching, forgiving, leading, and celebrating one another and me. May it always be so.

Special thanks to my amazing sister, Sue Trexler, for modeling KinKeeping for me all my life.

And special thanks also to my dear friend, Susan DeWenter, for her photography and design gifts, and constant inspiration.

Table of Contents

Introduction

Remember paperchains?
From early years on, people seem to enjoy making them.
A few pieces of colored paper, a little snip-snip here, a little glue or
paste or tape there, and soon a colorful chain, all interconnected,
lies in front of you.

I got a "C" in Art every quarter in elementary school no matter
how hard I tried. But I had a secret weapon to get one "A" out of
the class. I knew at Christmas we would choose groups and have a
paper chain contest—and my friends Barb, Karlys and Susan were
so good at it that, together, we would have a lot of fun and maybe
even have a chance to win and all of us earn an "A".

When the contest day came, we pushed our desks together, got
our supplies, and started. We used school paste on popsicle sticks,
brightly colored construction paper, and little brown paper towels
folded and almost dripping wet—to keep us from sticking together.
What fun, even when I forgot I had paste on my hand and brushed
my hair out of my face. As we chose our colors, cut and pasted, and
cooperated in connecting the loops, each one of us was important
in the project.

Together, we made A's, created a bunch of long, colorful paperchains—and stored a happy memory in our hearts. These girls were KinKeeping me, and I was KinKeeping them, nurturing the lovely connection we had.

Paperchains remind me of the connections contained in any circle of caring & love

... and, truly, we are connected in life in so many ways—across generations of families and friends, across geographic space, across peoples and cultures.

I believe that we choose our side of the quality of our connections, in part by the effort and intention we invest in the careful tending of the valuable relationships of our lives, both intimate and public.

And so I want to suggest that you think about the concept of KinKeeping. There's much more information on it at www. kinkeeping.com, and another book, KinKeeping 101, will be published soon.

For right now, I'd like to simply report on the origin of this word: **"KinKeepers"** was originally used to describe the older, often unmarried women in a family who spent time and effort helping to keep the generations connected—i.e., **KinKeeping**.

Upon learning of this in a college textbook, I immediately resonated with the word itself, as well as the idea. KinKeeping immediately became much more to me—much broader and much deeper.

I saw **KinKeeping** all around me—and I saw **Kin** as those **related to me by blood, by law, and by choice.** In modern times, more and more it seems we **choose** our families, we choose our kin, we choose those with whom we stay connected.

But stay connected we must! Humans are **hard-wired to connect**— and neuroscience is discovering more about this human need every day. We are not geared to live in isolation. Whether extroverted or introverted in personality type, we need other humans to connect to and with, at varying levels, for health.

It became apparent to me that we also need other connections— to our selves, to our higher power (whatever we call him or her), to our communities, to our nations, to our world. We need to be connected to the animal kingdom, and to the living plants on this planet—trees, grass, ground—Mother Earth herself. Deep calls to deep, and some among us connect to rocks and stones and matter that has been here much longer than any of us.

So I invite you to think about some of these concepts below:

- We can be KinKeepers to our **own soul.** Valuing the gift of life, we can choose to care for our selves, putting on our own oxygen masks first, in order to best move forward to fulfill our purpose on this earth—and so that we have life energy enough to help others.

- We can KinKeep the relationship we have with a **higher power**, however we address it/him/her—or if atheist, perhaps we can build connections with the **universe** around us. To nourish the spirit within us, we can reach beyond what we know and understand, always wanting to connect with the mysteries themselves.

- We can purposefully nurture our own **families**, **friends**, and other **KinGroups.**

- We can **help others connect** as we stretch out into our communities, making a difference in the lives of those around us.

- We can acknowledge the value of **each human life** on the earth—and the rich diversity among us.

- We can enjoy the richness of our connections to members of the **animal kingdom.**

- And always, we can honor our reliance upon **the good earth** and all of **nature's** brilliant and subtle, yet essential contributions to our lives.

By **acknowledging** and **strengthening** these **bonds** between us
and other people and things in our world, close and far,
we will be enriched ourselves,
while enriching others.

KinKept—Intentionally Nurturing Connections contains little stories from my life and the lives of many others. It includes times when somebody chose to KinKeep me—they reached out to me and let me know I was part of their circle of life.

The stories relate times when others helped me feel like I belonged, and like I MATTERED.

And some stories tell of my small efforts at KinKeeping others, in turn.

Still other stories are of times when I was just living my life and personally "came upon" or heard about someone else in the lovely act of KinKeeping—or someone told me their story and I knew the amazing value of the event and wanted to share it.

Perhaps, as you read these little stories, you'll start to be more conscious of the KinKeeping stories of your own life. Some questions may arise in your thinking, in your heart.

- What does it mean to you to **BELONG somewhere**, with someone, with others? To **fit in to a group** of any kind? To have a **partner**? A **best friend**?

- When did someone KinKeep you? **How did they do it?**

- **How did you feel** when they did it?

- Have you ever thanked them or let them know **how you were affected or are affected currently** by their thoughtful, caring inclusion of you?

- How have you **purposefully connected** with someone you care about? Have you KinKept others on purpose?

- What did you **invest** in them, in the relationship, that helped make it happen? Attention, time, energy, money, affirmation?

- **Was the cost worth the deepened connection?**

- What might you **do differently** next time?

- What ideas could you **share with others** to help them Kinkeep?

****

You are invited to **consider the concept of KinKeeping** in these pages as you read about how it was walked out or viewed in one person's real life. What you do with this concept is strictly up to you! Perhaps you'll have a little consciousness-raising on the topic—maybe you'll focus for a time on the KinKeeping in your world. Or notice when it occurs to you, for you, for others.

I'm hoping **KinKept** will help you think of and be renewed by your own unique history of **KinKeeping**, both as a receiver and as a giver.

Perhaps, as you think back on certain stories from your own history, you will be able to remember special times that just stuck in your soul, memories that still make you smile—or tear up—maybe those were moments of KinKeeping in action!

While humans in general have deep needs relating to connecting with others and belonging to various KinGroups, some among us have a deeper, intrinsic interest in KinKeeping; we were created with a compelling urge surrounding the need to connect.

Maybe you feel a desire to be more connected to friends and family in your own life, or to help others better connect to their own circles of family, friends, acquaintances, etc. Perhaps you will be refreshed and encouraged to think about purposefully enhancing the KinKeeping thoughts and activities you're probably already involved in.

You might want to refresh the lines of communication with some of your various KinGroups, reaching out to those you love and care about, reinvigorating a friendship or two, re-connecting with that book club, attending that reunion, or implementing any way of meaningfully connecting with someone else. You may plan a hiking trip to re-connect with the good earth, or develop a practice of self-care. You may take care to meditate, or worship your God in ways that are meaningful to you. You might adopt a pet, or go horseback riding. So many ways to connect!

As your awareness of KinKeeping opportunities and activities increases, you may also make the decision that it is worth your time to notice, value, treasure, and intentionally respond to the ways you are **KinKept** by others.

✷✷✷✷✷✷✷✷✷✷✷✷✷✷✷✷✷✷✷✷

IMPORTANT NOTE #1:

As you know, sometimes certain previously essential relationships with individuals or KinGroups can become simply toxic to us—and we would not be well served to attempt to strengthen connections there. It is wise to consider this season's needs of your own deep heart, perhaps seeking outside counsel before making any sort of KinKeeping Offer to those in that group. **KinKeepers for us are those who will value us, treasure the connection, and enrich our lives. If it's unhealthy for you to reach out to someone, don't do it. There are other connections you may need to strengthen at a given season in your life.**

IMPORTANT NOTE #2:

I have to preface this book by saying the obvious: **I'm not an expert on this topic.** I didn't even think up the name—I just saw it and loved it, and have expanded on it in my mind and heart over the years, being foolhardy enough to attempt to give the concept some shape and structure. I lay no claim to the concept whatsoever— others smarter, wiser, better than me have been doing magnificent KinKeeping all their lives. I bow to them and want to learn from them! I am very happy to acknowledge the thousands of people who have been KinKeepers to me in some form or other throughout my life, even when I felt lower than low and did not think anyone cared.

Always—someone reached out. Someone came along to KinKeep me. **I venture to suggest that each of us has been KinKept—** whether by our own selves, our higher power, another person, an animal, a restorative connection with the earth and nature— somehow we connected with something. We moved out of that paralyzing void of isolation and reached out, or were reached out to.

Perhaps we would not still be alive if that were not true. We need each other. **We need KinKeepers of all kinds among us!** I am just the beginner, the lowest among that group of folks who recognize the need for connection to thrive in life. But I'm an energetic, appreciative, excited KinKeeper—always looking to learn from others, and then to continue the practice of appropriately, intentionally KinKeeping to the best of my ability.

I hope you'll join me!

Kinkept

Intentionally
Nurturing Connection

... let the stories begin!

(no particular order)

That First Precious Kinkeeper
in My Life

*I am so privileged
to have been tutored
in KinKeeping by my
mother's fine example, and
by the fun she made of
connecting*

"Hey, kids! Have we got room for one more in the back seat?"

Of course, she started it all. My little mama, Doris Capp. Mom never saw a person to whom she didn't reach out. My youngest son once asked me, "So is that where you got that KinKeeping stuff, Mom? I remember Grandma Capp—no matter where we picked her up when she was living in Tulsa, she would always be sitting there waiting, talking to someone like they were her best friend. I remember asking her if she knew those people—and she always said, 'No. We just got to talking—Gosh, that was fun!'"

And that's what I have in my memory bank, too. When I was a little kid, riding with Mom along the gravel or freshly tarred roads in rural Minnesota or South Dakots, there was literally not one hitchhiker that we didn't pick up. And no matter what their circumstances were, by the time we dropped them off, they were giving Mom their address, scrawled on whatever scraps of paper we could find, and promising to stay in touch, and thanking her for sharing whatever we might have had in the car with us to eat.

All her life, whatever she had, food, money, energy, or time—and especially love—she would share. With anyone. She would reach out. My dad had a generous heart, as well - but Mom was in her own category on the KinKeeping scale.

Others reached back to her, as well, and she received so honestly, so graciously; her KinKeeping adventures went both ways. She KinKept her own with her very best efforts, and she KinKept the wide world every way she could, as well.

I'm so grateful to be my mother's daughter.

Continuing Traditions

A lesson is passed

to the next generation

on the proper

care and keeping

of the

"Junk Drawer Starter Kit"

"Will you do Millie for the shower?
Do Millie! Please, we love Millie!"

We urge my sister-in-law Cheryl to put on her old-style dress, tuck a hankie into her bosom, perch the granny glasses on her nose, tie on the grandma shoes, and pull up the knee-high nylons that fall halfway down her legs. Invited as surprise entertainment, Cheryl plays *"Millie"* sometimes for bridal showers, entering the gathering as if she's an old neighbor or friend.

She starts right in, pertly lecturing the women who sit next to her, telling them about proper etiquette that was expected in 1956.

She plays *"Millie"* as a mixture of someone's Great Aunt Flo and another's lovable, eccentric great-grandma, using skit lines that sound like they were taken verbatim from our own relatives.

Now our favorite part: *Millie* brings out her bridal gift, ready with a lesson on its proper use.

With a flourish worthy of a diva, she proudly removes the plastic Wal-Mart bag she has used as wrapping paper and ... ta da!

Old and young friends of the bride and groom all laugh together as *Millie* shows the grinning bride where to save those twisties from the bread wrappers, that set of old keys, twirly-topped toothpicks from a long-ago party, little skewers to put in the corn-on-the-cob, and other assorted "treasures".

Millie has just ensured that one new bride can some day pass on the time-honored tradition of the Junk Drawer.

Sharing Resources/Memories

... in so many ways,
we are linked
to our past,
to our history,

to our kin

It's 1965. I am in my teens. And kind of hungry.
I am hoping there's something substantial for supper.

Times are tough on our little farm in the lake country of
Minnesota.

My parents are struggling—and so are us kids.

Suddenly, whose car is that, coming down the road, looking like it's
going to turn in our driveway?

Oh, I'm excited. It's our Uncle Stanley and Aunt Anna, and cousin
Mary Jane. And all of us kids know what that means. We run out to
the car to greet them.

And then we line up to lug in the plenty they always bring, along
with their suitcases: plenty of Bohemian kolaches, plenty of fresh
homemade bread, plenty of hot dish, North Dakota sausage,
venison, and big pans of cakes, cookies, and bars!

That night after chores are done and we've shared a delicious
meal with our relatives, we enjoy another kind of plenty: plenty
of boisterous storytelling about all the family we haven't seen in a
while. Sometimes there will even be Czech songs my dad and his
brother sing together, rekindling memories from their childhood.

Tonight we all give our guests our beds; we sleep on quilts on the
floor and we are happy and full—

The world is a safer place when we know
we have Kinfolks who will share their plenty with us.

Sharing Resources/Memories

We kids love the help with
our chores,

we love sharing these
KinKeepers' plenty,

and we love the support
we feel just from their

presence

Now it is morning, and Uncle Stanley goes out for chores with us, helping milk the cows and feed the calves, slop the pigs and scatter grain for the chickens. Aunt Anna and cousin Mary Jane help my mom cook more food, mixing up pancakes with flour made from the spring wheat grown on their own homestead, and we swirl butter with homemade jam my aunt has made from chokecherries growing wild on the back forty of their farm.

Breakfast is a delight of food and talk, some happy, some serious. All day the work goes on, and the talking goes on, inside and outside. After the evening's milking and supper, the "boys" all head for the horseshoe pit and the women get comfortable in the house, laughing and talking for hours. These visits feed our souls.

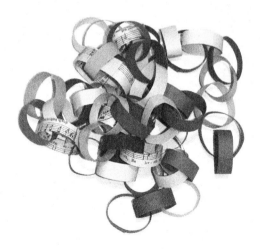

Enduring Friendships
Across Lines of Hardship

I am not alone,

after all

The soccer game is just starting. I have struggled to make myself come alone, now that most of them know we are divorced.

I park and trudge toward the field, knowing my boys will be watching to see if Mom is there to cheer them on.

As I round the corner and head for the sidelines, Geri waves at me to come sit beside her and a couple other moms with my folding chair.

I smile, relieved, and head her way.

She reaches for my hand, holds it just a moment, and says, *"We're still here, Judy, you'll get through this.*

Hang in there, girl."

It is enough for now.
This KinKeeper's words and actions help me know:
I will survive.

Being a Good Neighbor

We are part of a community.

They have let us in

The knock is loud on the door down below. I'm surprised—
I didn't hear the car drive in.
"I'll go," I say, so I head down the stairs
trying to get a look out the window in the front door.

With beaming faces, it's our new neighbors, a box in their hands.

Produce from their beautiful garden—green beans, zucchini, onions, leeks—even a small vase with fresh-cut flowers from the tall, beautiful bushes we see when we drive by their farmhouse!

They live a quarter-mile from us, and their house is a bit back in the trees, but we can hear their rooster, Mr. Big, crowing loudly in the summer mornings (in the summer afternoons, in the summer evenings, too) and he always reminds us we are part of a community.

Enjoying their friendly conversation, and later, that good food and the heady scent and beauty of the homegrown flowers, I am more at rest in this new living quarters.

My heart knows they have let us in, accepted us as neighbors, maybe friends, opened their hearts to us.

When we drive by and honk—and they wave back,
it feels good to be connected and KinKept
in our own neighborhood.

Volunteering to Help Others
Reminding each other we are not alone

There are places—
There is someone who will
catch him if he falls—
There are people who care
enough to donate food,
to volunteer time,
to let him know
he is not alone

"Glad to meet you. And yes, I work here," the woman behind the counter at the Food Shelf said to Benny.

"I always volunteer here on Thursdays after I get off at my regular job. I depended on this place to get my kids and me through a hard time a couple years ago, so I decided when I was better off, I'd do what I could to give back to help someone else.

"What is it that you need? We have lots of cereal right now, some meat, and some canned goods. We can help get you through whatever you're dealing with."

"Yeah," he answered, looking at the floor.

"We don't have much and the kids are really hungry."

She sent him home with a couple of big boxes full of wholesome food, enough for a week for him and his three kids. He thanked her, his voice cracking as he struggled to control his emotions.

The children will not cry themselves to sleep tonight; their bellies will be full. He will hope again.

Businesses invested in Communities

We are connected to a
business community
who tries to
KinKeep
their customers
and neighbors;
they are standing
with us

It's hailing outside. Again.
Dark skies in the middle of the summer day, and thousands of
staccato, bouncing balls of ice hitting the ground.

Daddy's face is grim and drawn; he's pacing back and forth by the
windows in the living room.

What will we do? If the crops are ruined, how will we go on?

I'm old enough to know about the seed money we borrowed that
must be paid back at harvest. If everything is ruined in this storm,
we could lose our home.

Will we be kicked out on the gravel road, will we have to leave the
farm, the only home we know?

Weeks later, I walk beside my parents as they leave the lender's
office in town. I can feel the tension in my dad has lessened; his
step is lighter. They're giving us more time to make payments. We
don't have to move .

Our community has stood by us.

Sharing Space in Transition Times

These KinKeepers
hold me always in the
bosom of their heart
and their home

"You know you can live with us any time you need to, Judy.
We've got room and we can make it work."

Single at 45, with kids still to raise and raging emotions to manage, twice I spend time living in the basement of the home of my sister, Sue, her husband Ray and family while I figure out a next move.

They are veteran KinKeepers, already caring for my mother after her stroke, and they make both of us feel welcome and wanted, even necessary.

Together with their two children and a little dog named Jellybean, we all make a family, a group of kin.

We each do our part: we cook, clean, hold jobs, go to school, and care for each other. When I'm in the way, or require extra effort, they never act like it. When I'm ready to move on, they tell me they will miss me.

As long as Ray and Sue are alive,
I know I am not alone.

Valuing the Vulnerable

Being cared for
is not a language
he knows yet;
it will take time and
repeated care and
love before his heart
can translate
those words

Ronnie is adopted, from an orphanage in Europe. He has trouble connecting with anyone; he had no mother or father to teach him about life in his earliest years.

Feeling alone in the world, he has problems trusting anyone.

His new mom and dad do not give up.

They are not naïve, they are not ignorant, neither are they superhuman. So they struggle as they work to KinKeep him and to teach him what love means, and why it will help him if he can learn to trust someone.

He finishes tightening the bolt, frowns slightly, looks up tentatively, fearfully to see if it's going to be okay.

"You've done it right, Ronnie, good job," his new dad says.

Ronnie nods, a little satisfied, a little reassured, not quite ready to accept and trust the praise, but he can kind of hear it, at least this time.

Being cared for is not a language he knows yet; it will take time and repeated care and love before his heart can translate the words. But every smile, every kind word matters—and builds his new vocabulary.

Soon he will understand that he is being KinKept.

Making Friends into Kin

*She remembers
the way
our family was
family to her*

Remember me? I got to babysit you
quite often when you were just a little girl,
an old soul in a young body.
You were the most amazing, wonderful child—
enormous eyes, a bright and shining heart,
even at two.
You captured *my* heart
and I will never forget you.

She is now 13 and she remembers *me*!

She remembers waving sparklers outside my house on New Years' Eve when she was 3 years old, she remembers me reading *The Giving Tree* to her, over and over.

She laughs as she recalls lots of KinKeeping moments—making cookies with me, watching soccer games with our family, wrestling with my sons on the floor, and being loved by my daughter who dated her dad.

We loved her, and love her still.

We are connected to her in this world

and we hope to keep on

KinKeeping her.

KinGroups

*They have not been alone
in their walk through life*

Still they gather. Lovely and lively and more bonded as the years advance, the women who comprise this strong KinGroup are still full of energy, wisdom and humor.

Originally a group of 9, they are now 8; one has passed away. They are the essence of sisterhood, though not related by blood. For over 25 years, they've been kith and kin to one another.

Together, they have been KinKeepers to each other's lives and families, celebrating countless rites of passage along the way: birthdays, graduations, weddings, baby showers. And sharing the hard times, too, including illness and death.

Now in their grandma years, they start the cycle again, with renewed and multiplied vigor, and fresh eyes for the beauty of the new lives all around them.

Truly joys are multiplied and sorrows divided when shared with the group. Each has been KinKept, each is a KinKeeper.

They have the essence of wealth:

They have not been alone in their walk through life.

Standing with our Kin

I am sad,
but their solidarity helps

I feel linked
to people who care

Fifteen and horse-crazy, I am in love only with my
American Saddle-Bred horse, King.

I have no clue how my parents were able to justify spending $150 on an animal that would not produce milk, meat, or eggs for our farm family, but somehow they have, knowing what he means to me. And I have been allowed to spend time working with him in the freshly mown alfalfa field, preparing for the county fair's horse show contest.

My neighbor, Jeanne, has offered to lend me her horse trailer to transport King to town for the horse show—a marvelous, generous offer that has made all the work of practicing riding exciting, hopeful and goal-oriented.

It's the day of the show. BUT—King will not—will NOT—be induced to enter the horse trailer. I am heartbroken. Jeanne and my dad spend over 2 hours with the sun beating down, helping me try to get him to walk up the ramp. We try everything! It's now too late to ride him the 13 miles into town ...

We all stand in the hayfield. Jeanne, not usually demonstrative with me, puts her arm around my shoulder. *"I'm sorry,"* she says. Daddy looks the other way to let my tears stay hidden. I'll have my big cry when I'm alone. I'll take off King's halter and let him back into his pasture. I'll be able to let this go and move on.

And long years later, I'll still remember these moments.
I will cherish having been KinKept in a Minnesota alfalfa field on
a hot, frustrating autumn day when hopes were dashed,

but hearts were knit.

45

Succor in Time of Sickness

He starts breathing
better. We all
start breathing better

We've been KinKept.
in all kinds
of ways in this crisis

We live in Kansas City, 5 hours away from family in
Tulsa and 10 hours from family in Minnesota.
Our son, Brian, is 3 and very ill—
high fever, deep cough, bronchitis.

I'm working fulltime, my husband is in college fulltime,
we are burning the candle at both ends in efforts to find ways to
trade off time to be there with Brian. We pray, hover and hold our
breath.

And then the KinKeepers start arriving.

A knock on the door of our third-floor walk-up attic apartment:
Brian's daycare provider has come by with a game, a toy and a book
for him. Our landlord stops in to see if there's anything he can do. A
Sunday School teacher brings us hot dish for supper.

My mother sends us a check for $20—now we can buy fresh fruit
for him.

And my mother-in-law drives into the scary big city by herself,
coming to stay with us for three days to help him get through it, to
help us get through it.

He starts breathing better.
We all start breathing better.
We've been KinKept.

Every Kid Matters—
Affirming Brotherhood

We're all

in

this

together

The brown paper bag holding the apples tears apart as the teenaged box-boy grabs it.

Apples fall everywhere, rolling, skittering, scattering, wide and far. His face turns bright red, he stammers out that he's sorry, he'll pick them right up.

Some of these apples will bruise from the fall, but I know immediately that I could bruise one young tender life even more if I don't handle this right. I have a chance to be a KinKeeper for this lad.

"No problem," I grin, as I bend down to grab the apples at my feet. *"Sometimes stuff just happens, no big deal. I think we'll be able to find them all. Thanks for collecting them so quickly. You're doing a great job!"*

He's less wary now, but keeps looking around as he picks up the apples, to see if anyone else is watching us. The checkout lady follows my lead and waves her hand dismissively. *"Sure, happens all the time, do you need us to replace any of those apples, ma'am?"* I shake my head, the boy ducks his head.

"Thanks," he says.

"No problem," I say.
"We're all in this together."

Embracing Immigrants

As long as there are
KinKeepers like her in
this world, newcomers
to any land can make
connections and find their
way to a better future

She's on the short side, tiny, cute
and sassy. Of Guatemalan descent,
she's American-born.

Remembering the struggles of her family during her own childhood,
she works in Immigration at the YWCA, helping others get their
visa and passport paperwork completed.

"This is my passion," she says.
"I love this work!"

With a college degree in graphic design, she was corking along in
corporate America—but wanted more out of her life. The pay cut
did not bother her; she would adjust.

Her eyes glisten as she tells of comforting and assisting newcomers
to this land, and watching as the fear in their eyes diminishes, and
they settle in to a new life with new opportunities, new friends, and
new hope.

I remember that my own grandparents once had the courage
to leave their native Czechoslovakia and get on a boat, risking
everything to try to make a better life out of their time on this earth.

I hope someone like this lovely woman, someone with her spirit,
her kindness, her empathy greeted them at Ellis Island.

Mental Health Assistance

Maybe his world
and those in it
will not come apart—
for today, anyway...

He is terrified. He has that deer-in-the-headlights look in his eyes and he's frozen mid-task. He's just four and recently diagnosed as autistic; he processes information differently than others. He's in a special-needs HeadStart pre-school class and he doesn't like it one bit. Not yet.

He's supposed to sit quietly in the circle while the teacher tells the group what the next task will be. Frustrated and confused, he starts keening loudly, moving his head from side to side, trying to ignore the instructions, making his own noise to shut out the teacher's noise.

She nods softly to a personal care assistant, who slowly, casually comes alongside him, sitting down, then carefully reaching out to try to snuggle him in next to her as she talks gently, quietly and slowly in his ear, telling him he'll be okay, and won't they have fun when they go outside to play in a minute.

Usually resistant to being touched, this time he is able to let her get close to him; now he can stop keening and calm down a bit. He starts to breathe normally and soon he can quietly listen to the teacher from the safety of the assistant's arms, even though he looks at the floor.

Thanks to KinKeepers who are trained, caring teachers and assistants, maybe he'll make it through the rest of the classtime without another meltdown.

Maybe his world and those in it will not come apart—for today anyway...

Protecting the Children

KinKeeping

and

KinKeepers

matter ...

"That is not okay," he says sternly to the boy's mother. *"You will not abuse this child any more. Law enforcement is on their way to deal with you. Darin will be taken to a shelter."*

Darin pulls his arms in tight, protecting his body. Even though the social worker is there by his side, when Momma is mad, anything can happen; he dares not even look at her face.

Momma is smart, and she's thinking fast, figuring out how to regain control, now that she knows Darin has just spilled the beans at school, telling first his teacher and then the social worker about the beating that morning. *"Do you think I did that?—oh, no,"* she says. *"He fell down the steps—he's a clumsy one, and he's always hurting himself. Just look at all his bruises—that boy is a klutz."*

In his head, Darin is screaming. *No! Please! Don't believe her!*

He starts to shake, and cannot stop. He knows what will happen if she convinces them. But instead, people believe *him.* The cops arrive. Momma is taken away, and the social worker takes him to the safe place.

It's not perfect, but he is staying alive
and his outside wounds are healing.

Now Darin has lots of KinKeepers in his world,
even though he misses Momma.

He may have a chance to start to heal emotionally
if his world can remain stable for a while.

Social Services Helpers

He asked for help and got it

Why can't he make his kids mind any more? Why won't they listen to him? What terrible thing is going to happen next? Jack knows he has lost control in his own household. And what on earth will that little tyrant be like when he is 17 instead of 6, anyway?

Jack admits he had started running around too much when Stacey left him and the kids, and the kids had kind of gone their own way, taking care of themselves as best they could. He's stopped drinking now and is home more—but the kids are usually either gone or fighting like crazy or talking smack to him. And that makes him mad, and so most of the time there is a regular three-ring circus going on at his house.

When the principal called about Alice missing too much school, Jack was just desperate enough that he told the truth. *"I'm losing it,"* he said. He asked for help and got it.

He went to counseling. He learned family skills. He learned to apologize when he was wrong. He learned how to manage his anger. He learned how to have fun with the whole family. He started making good, happy memories with the kids.

Jack stays in touch with the counselor, the family skills trainer, the principal. These KinKeepers surrounded him with assistance and made a difference in his life.

Things are better now at Jack's house— he's accepted being KinKept by others, and he's working at being a KinKeeper for his own family.

Professional Support

Always holding me in their back pocket, always there for me, always telling me the truth, and teaching me how to do better

"I can be a writer," I said. *"I'll do any of that kind of work
the Sales Team needs done—I love it."*
So Kathleen kindly gave me some tasks
and liked what she saw.
*"Have our head writers review your work
and edit it,"* she said.

And man alive, did they edit. For weeks and weeks, my work came
back with more red marks than black ink on the pages.

And every time I marched right back to Steve and Jen for help,
and they took time with me. They explained what I was missing,
showed me how to change it, praised me when I got it right.

And cheered me on when I got the job on the Training Team, as a
writer.

Always holding me in their back pocket,
always there for me,
always telling me the truth,
and teaching me how to do better.

KinKeepers of the first order—high on my list—
they let me join their ranks and instead of protecting their own
turf, they nurtured and celebrated me.

I am humbled and honored to be included
and kept close by those
whose work I admire.

KinKeeping Across Lines of Difference

Learning to KinKeep Each Other

He was "other." She was "different." They were "not like us."

We all look different, we have different cultures, we act differently, we have different struggles. Surely, we have many similar issues and challenges—but many among us have extra hurdles to overcome, simply because of the hand we are dealt at birth.

We all come with genetic packages, and we all arrive into cultural packages. Helpful or Difficult. But OURS. And each of those packages rains all over all of our lives; they shape us, form us, afflict us, gift us, and flow through us like water through a sieve, affecting all we touch, all we become. Making us each unique.

I am beginning to see the work involved in learning and practicing KinKeeping across these lines of diference. I've had some great role models - and some inadequate ones. Even after paying close attention to those good ones, I fail often. The deep respect I have for others is what I fall back upon. I want so badly to keep learning how to stretch across that which divides us!

So I will keep trying. I will keep learning and doing. Many of you KinKeepers are way ahead of me and I hope to learn from your KinKeeping ways. Because even with all the clumsy, awkward, ignorant missteps I make as I reach across those lines of difference in my learning journey, my heart cares. My heart wants to connect.

So I am going to stumble onward, owning my self and learning to be the best "me" I can be, making the best of my genes and my cultural heritage. I will continue to care about others and KinKeep as best I can.

I hope you will, too. We can do better.
Let's keep on learning together.

Generosity of Friendship

When I cannot drive
to my own
hearth and home,
I am still at home
in the home
of my friend

For no good reason, she opens her heart to me. We weren't even friends yet, although we both soon knew we would be.

The second time I ever talked to her, she heard I was going to need a place to stay in town during the week, and she said, *"Well, you must stay with me. I have room, we'll have fun, you must come. Don't get an efficiency, come stay with me."*

Crazy deal. How could it work?

But it does. Two to three days a week, I share her house in the city. And do we ever have fun.

We talk for hours, we craft together, we write and read and watch movies and share dinner. We have become dearest friends.

For no good reason, Carol KinKeeps me.

It is an unearned gift of such grace and kindness,

and it brings me much joy.

Professional Cameraderie

I receive the grace,
value the mercy,
and enjoy the ride,
learning everything
I can from this
KinKeeper's example,
her words,
and her actions

Coming alongside me as a friend as we teach parenting skills to precious, hurting families, Chris has my back. She helps me survive and succeed.

She is the young pup, the hotshot at the top of her game. She can de-escalate the toughest of emotional meltdowns with a look or perfectly placed move.

She is respected by everyone I know, whether a kid needing help and direction and boundaries, an out-of-control or overwhelmed parent, a teacher or court official.

Why she mentored me, I know not. She became friend to this new-kid-on-the-block when I am fifty-something in a new career, and she watches my back. She helps me out of hard situations, gives me suggestions on how to handle things, and makes sure I know she will be there for me.

She loves to laugh at my "old-lady" ability to blush when she jokingly invites me to see the risqué men's theater group, and I love to show her some tricks on the computer.

When new colleagues look to the heart and push past other differences, true collaboration and friendships can arise, make a workplace better, and enrich lives.

Gold-Standard KinKeeping

Day after Day,
these KinKeepers
enrich our world,
trying to make
it safe
for all

She's a world-class kinkeeper.
To me, my sister Sue is the Gold Standard for
standing in the gap and connecting people
of all kinds to life itself.

She can never turn even one away. She has the biggest heart of anyone I know.

Her name should be Mother Sue-Teresa. She cares for all, every single one that ever crosses her path. She's not an undisciplined softie, though. Just try hurting anyone around her and you will see the fire of Elijah coming to put you in your place and snatch any victims right out of your clutches.

She helps victims of abuse. In every way they need help. She holds their hand, holds their respect, holds them in her heart as they tell their stories, as they dare to speak their truths. She holds their children as they cry and sob and dare to change their lives.

She sits with them in court, faces down their abusers without ever a flinch. She drives them back to their homes while they grab clothes to start a new life. She helps them move into temporary emergency housing.

She finds new clothes for them, she brings them food, she just plain loves them. She gives her life for them.

She'd do it for free.
According to her, she's nothing special;
her co-workers do it all, too.

Our world is better because of these advocates for humanity.

Animal KinKeepers

The Chain of Life ...
extends to the animals

Dan's back deck is a haven, full of colorful birds of all kinds. There's a reason—he feeds them!—all the time.

His birdbath is always clean and ready with water. He watches their little birdfights, and makes sure the food is where they can reach it. He cleans up after them every day—keeping the seed fresh and the perches cleared off.

When winter comes and snow falls, look out your back window! Dan is out there as soon as he can be. He's filling the feeders right away, hanging suet, and caring for the birds. Even the tiny sparrows have a special place to go, and food to sustain them. Happy creatures, happy songs!

I can hear those happy songs
because
Dan makes a difference,
because Dan KinKeeps
these fellow inhabitants
of Planet Earth,
helping them
stay connected to life,
as they enrich and brighten our world.

KinGroup Connecting

I'm glad
when Jamie calls

Jamie's KinKeeping
keeps me connected

A couple of times a year, the phone rings and it's Jamie. *"Just checking up on you,"* he says. *"Did you hear that Cassie got remarried last month? And did you know Sam just ran for mayor and got it? Can you imagine?"*

Then he's off and running, asking about me and all the class members from way back that I know of—what's the old group gotten themselves up to now? Has anybody made their first million yet—and remember what Mr. Anders used to say about how to manage your first million, back in high school accounting class?

And who could forget when the principal tripped on that block and fell into the pool with all his clothes on! And Jamie just rattles on and on, and sometimes I'm bored silly—and sometimes it's just the nicest connection to all those people I used to know and who influenced and moderated the angst of my school years.

Knowing what people are up to, and getting to hear that the popular guy is still a nice person and stayed friendly—sometimes it's satisfying to hear that. Without Jamie's calls, I would have lost connection to these classmates.

We're both careful that our conversation doesn't just turn into gossip—we make plans to get together with others and to include as many as we can.

It has to start with someone—some KinKeeper—taking the time to keep the connections warm and nurturing.

Reunions

It always takes someone with a KinKeeper's heart to make any kind of reunion happen

Rain down some blessings on Martha and her crew!

Every year she pulls out the address lists, updates them, gets the
planners together starts the ball rolling.

When plans are finalized, she prints out the High School Reunion
invitations and agendas.

Martha always hosts the addressing get-together and carries the
envelopes to the post office. Her group confirms the date with the
restaurant, gets the music ready and books the entertainment.

Then they get all dolled up, drag their dates and husbands along,
and go make the high school reunion happen.

Relationships are renewed,

life transitions are reviewed,

connections to each other's shared history are validated

and a foundation in life is affirmed—

thanks to the KinKeepers among us.

Spotlighting Connections
Between the Generations

I didn't even realize I was KinKeeping my friend, nurturing her and her mom

It's Kristi's mom—visiting from out of town. I'd rather just have lunch with Kristi, but since her mom is here, that will be fun, too, and all three of us will go out together.

Not too bad, kind of nice conversation. Fun to hear about Kristi when she was little.

I notice her mom's pretty skin and I say, *"Kristi—I'm looking at the future and the future is looking good!"* Kristi smiles and looks proudly at her mom.

Little do I know that her mother will tuck that tiny compliment in her head and her heart, and it will help buffer her when she feels herself starting to grow old. She will remember that a sassy, twenty-something New Yorker thought she looked pretty good— and that has some meaning to her, gives her confidence and makes her smile, more than once, as she remembers the setting and the comment.

Nor do I have any idea that Kristi will also remember it and look forward to keeping good skin and her own sense of beauty as she gets older. Somehow, I've helped her to be thankful for this element of her heritage.

I didn't realize my words would have much meaning to either of them. I didn't understand that I was KinKeeping my friend, nurturing her and her mom.

I just pointed out a connection I saw
and offered a compliment.

Animal KinKeepers

*I think we are now family
and it's going to be
all right*

CAT TALK

I had no clue what kind of heaven we were landing in when they came to pick us up! We had an owner who loved cats, and especially us, but sometimes he would just disappear and we'd have to stay with some stranger we didn't even like.

We couldn't stay in our own bed at night, we didn't like the strange new place we'd have to live in, and it was just getting worse and worse because of our owner's travelng. Monster, my friend, seemed to be getting sick a lot. Life was just not so good for us kittycats any more.

SO—When Susie and Bruce came to pick us up, we both knew right away it would be a good thing. But wow, meowww! It's actually awesome! We hit the jackpot! They love us already—smile whenever they see us, hold us and pet us a lot, and give us the run of the house. That Susie! She is such a KinKeeper! She just always is looking for some nice new thing she can do that might make us even happier. She takes pictures of us, she cuddles us, she makes sure we eat like kings, she even took time off work to be with us the first two days we were at her house, just so we wouldn't be lonely!

Things are REALLY looking up for me and Monster, and so that's why I got scared when he climbed up the drapes and pushed up the ceiling tile and got into the ceiling space. Susie and Bruce looked for him and called for him and got all worried and I was so afraid they'd be mad—but when they found him peeking down at them, they just hugged him and hugged him, and so I think we are now family and it's going to be all right.

Now, if they would just let me outside so I could chase those darn chirpy little robins!

Embracing the Newbies

*It feels like we didn't
do much, but she says
our KinKeeping
means a lot*

She's newly hired here, and I can tell she's smart enough, but oh my, there's so much new stuff to learn. I'm sure she gets tired of asking questions. It's hard to be the new one and have to feel ignorant for a while.

I'm going to stay patient and be as much help to her as I can be. I remember being new; I know how I appreciated the kindness of the one who trained me, and the others in the office.

I introduce her to the group down the hall and they all try to be nice, but they have their own jobs to do and not much extra time. Still, I can tell it matters to her that they always say hello and ask how it's going for her.

Shortly after she started work here, her mother died. Wow, what do you say to someone you don't really know yet, when a big thing like that happens? We didn't really know how to KinKeep her through that—but at least we all got together and sent her a plant and a card to make sure she knew we cared. I hope it helped.

She brightens up when she mentions that it's still growing and it reminds her of her mom and of all of us.

She has to miss a bit of work for the funeral and I'm glad I can pitch in and cover for her duties. Sure, I'm busy and it makes me really stretch to get it done, but I like her and I'll do it as long as she needs me to.

I just know how I would feel if it was me, having to make the adjustment to a new job, and to losing my mom. I want to help anyway I can.

Somebody's got to make the effort; I'm glad I did!

Rites of Passage

How important
for KinKeepers
to be witnesses to
rites of passage,
transition times,
commemorating
of accomplishments

"Where is Brian? I can't see him, Mother—where did it say he would be?" I am sad that I can't help my daughter
find her brother.

Binoculars would have helped, but of course, I didn't think to bring any with me on our trip to San Diego. We have saved and planned, made arrangements for everything else in our lives, and excitedly brought the kids to see Brian graduate from Marine Corps training. I didn't think about the size of his squadron, the huge playing field, and how far away our seats would be. So I can't see him, either!

There's just a huge group of ramrod-straight, parade-dressed, marching-exactly-together young Marines performing as we watch.

And then the ceremony is over, the Marines are dismissed, and MY Marine is walking toward us. Finally it's really him, in person— we're seeing him for the first time in months. His brothers and his sister run to him, and just grab him and hug him—we have missed him while he's been away! A military hug for his dad and me, then he must proudly introduce us to his Drill Sergeant—

I hear his voice trembling, and his heart saying, '*This is where I come from, these are my people, I have roots*.'

How important for KinKeepers to be witnesses to rites of passage, transition times, commemorating of accomplishments.

Although we could not stand next to him through this difficult time of training, we have stood behind him. We are proud— so PROUD—of him and all that he has accomplished.
And we're here to cheer him on.

Family Gatherings

Having regular
gatherings
helps everyone
stay in touch

"The cousins are here, the cousins are here!"

And out the door the little kids run; they can't wait to get started playing. Another car pulls in right behind the first one—more cousins!

It's the monthly birthday gathering for the Olsons. This month, three people have had birthdays—the baby of the group has turned two, and it's her mama's birth month, as well. And the patriarch is now 63—and happy to see the cars starting to arrive. Mom has made a birthday cake and Aunt Alice is putting 3 candles on it— one for each person who's having a birthday.

The family depends on this time set aside to celebrate, to connect, to KinKeep each other. Having regular gatherings helps everyone stay in touch. There's the chance to touch base, say hi and see what's been going on in others' lives. Jane has brought a new boyfriend along; Sam has a friend spending the night who comes with him.

From his comfy recliner, Grandpa watches the group talking, cooking, playing games, gathering around the football game on tv, cousins outside running around and screaming like banshees in the yard, and he nods, grinning, to himself. For him, this is the best day of every month.

Even tightly knit families need the reinforcement of KinKeeping gatherings and activities. KinGroups of every kind flourish and grow strong when members are able to see each other and connect regularly.

And when it's not possible to do that in person, there's always texting, calling, Facebook and ... even snail mail.

Family Gatherings

*They are
KinKeeping their papa,
risking, sacrificing,
spending time, effort, and
money—all for him*

"You can do it, Sue—calm and steady, take one small and careful step at a time. See, you're one of us—you can do it."

Sue, in her fifties, is high in the air, up on a roof—for the first time ever. She's afraid of heights, but has come, out of love, to join the rest of her relatives, shingling Dad's roof as a family project.

Everything in her screams: *get down, get off this roof, you're going to die doing this foolhardy thing*—but—she's got Benson blood in her! And if the rest of them can do this, so can she.

And so she does. By afternoon's end, the roof is shingled, brand spankin' new, and she's as comfy up there as her siblings—an accomplished roofer!

Cheers go up—the crew is all on the ground now, and there's her dad, tears in his eyes, pride and gratitude written on his face. His kids came through! They did it! He can safely stay in his house a while longer, stay in his life as he has known it. Having them to thank only makes it sweeter.

When this group says they love him, he knows they mean it.

A day spent, a lasting roof, a forever memory.

KinGroup Talent Show

The circle of safety will nurture many fine talents

Kicky, smart, self-assured, they begin ringing the doorbell at 6:30 pm sharp. Some bring guitar cases, one has a violin, one carries sheet music for the piano in the living room.

It's Talent Show night in the big house in Tulsa, and the microphone and speakers are all set up. Homemade bread is rising in the kitchen, a vegetarian entrée is cooking in the oven, and invited friends and participants are ready to roll.

Every couple of months, someone in the group hosts the Talent Show, and it's never certain who enjoys it more—those who come to perform, or those who come to clap and cheer. Of course, some come just to eat! The big idea is that everyone gets together with the chance to test their creative powers on a friendly audience.

They give—we receive—we're all KinKeeping each other! We whistle, we clap, we swoon, we remark to each other on the courage and skills of the performers. They sing, they play instruments, they read poems, they display their art, they share home-crafted videos—they blush, they shine, they dare, they succeed.

It's all good. The circle of safety will nurture many fine talents that will either go on to bless the wide world, or perhaps be enjoyed mainly in these home circles.

By intentionally supporting each other,
we create a warm, rich haven for creative gifts to flourish.

Mentoring

She starts out believing
the best of people and
watches them rise to
become that best

"Let's role-play how you'll handle that situation, Patti. I've seen you do a great job with her before, and I know you've got it in you to manage this problem."

"Okay, I'm Dr. Olson, and I have a problem with my nurse. I'll start—you respond, and I'll coach you if I think you would be better off to go a different direction with this critical conversation."

Michele always thinks the best of people, in both her personal and professional lives. She's a KinKeeper, always giving friends and employees the benefit of the doubt—and she always believes in them, gives them chances for do-overs whenever she can. She models the best in management techniques, and she's always willing to step in and coach people, too.

She thinks it's normal—she just calls it using her common sense, treating people as she would like to be treated herself.

But she passes it on, to anyone who asks. And she takes care to pass it on in a respectful way that acknowledges the skills the person already has and builds on them. And behind the scenes, more KinKeeping goes on: she prays for those she counsels, she sends little notes, she takes time for coffee, always building relationship, always extending a hand.

Her friendships go better, and her business goes better,
because she starts out believing the best of people
and watches them rise to become that best.

Maintaining Heritages

Cheryl KinKeeps me by generously sharing the fruits of her ongoing KinKeeping of the family's perennial flowers

I have always loved peonies, and I'm often nostalgic for the pinkish-white hues that grew in my mother's garden on the old farmplace in Minnesota where I grew up.

Somehow that smell and the beauty I perceive in the rich, heavy blooms are just enough to call back so many precious memories. Memories of the talks Mother and I shared, me sitting on the red and chrome high stool in the kitchen, her by the table, often peeling potatoes or stirring up cookies. And so often, that heavenly peony smell coming in the open window at my back.

Twice I transplanted some from Mother as I moved around the nation, but finally they had to be left behind.

Now Cheryl has a surprise for me. *"Come over—this afternoon, right away. It's time to divide some perennials—and I remember you love peonies!"*

And so now my own yard holds many transplanted treasures—thanks to them having been carefully KinKept by Cheryl's kindness and respect for heritage and memories. Peonies and daylilies—passed along over many, many years, some known to have been in Cheryl's family since the early 1900's. Riches indeed.

Cheryl KinKeeps me by generously sharing the fruits of her ongoing KinKeeping of the family perennial flowers. Soon I will smell my own stash of these precious peonies, and one day, perhaps be privileged to send home their fragrance with my own children.

Kinkeeping the treasures of Mother Earth helps me KinKeep the lovely memories I have of my own mother.

Connecting Others

My friend is having fun being a part of helping people connect with each other

My friend has mentioned it several times—we're kind of new around here, and she thinks we need to meet her brother and his wife, we would have a lot in common with them and maybe begin a cool friendship.

Ah, you never know—sometimes that kind of stuff works, and sometimes it doesn't. So I guess we'll just see if it ever happens. No big deal, I'm thinkin'.

The phone rings with a KinKeeping offer—*"Weren't you going to stop by this afternoon? My brother is here and I so hope you can come while he and his wife are here!"* Well, okay.

So we came, and we had a great time!

Wow, the talk just won't stop! We have so much in common, it's like we've really had similar experiences, and it's fun getting to know them. They're going to follow us home so we can share some special seeds, and I want to see if her brother knows what is wrong with one of my chickens, and then we're already talking about getting together again.

Happy face on the couch, just watching the four of us talk—my friend is having fun being a part of helping people connect with each other. I know it's up to my husband and me, and her brother and his wife, if this KinKeeping event goes any further.

But I can already see the twinkle in my friend's eye, and I feel the chain of connection growing; now it feels even more like it's our home, and our community.

Family Caring

Sometimes KinKeeping is about respecting each other, maybe only nudging people toward better choices in tiny baby steps, at the rate the KinKept one can accept and absorb.

"I wish he'd eat right and take care of himself," she said as she shook her head and pursed her lips. *"He's my dad and I love him—but this is his second heart thing and nothing's changed from before. He's just not ready to make a switch in his lifestyle."*

My young friend is visibly upset. Her dad is in intensive care in another city and she's making plans to go there to spend her weekend sitting at his bedside. She doesn't begrudge him her time—no, this KinKeeper is just truly sad he's continuing to make the decisions he's always made, decisions many of my generation have made: to ignore exercise, eat unhealthy foods, work too much and rest too little. What will be the end of this story? Next time will she be rushing to his deathbed?

At his hospital bedside, she tries. She mentions all the things his doctor is telling him he needs to do differently. He looks at her, he seems to listen, she does not know what is sinking in—or if anything is. But she tries. And for Christmas, she's all excited as she is bringing him and her mom each a wrapped-up Fitbit. Maybe that will get them both going the right direction. They could keep track of their activities and start making better lifestyle decisions.

"Well, my mom is using the Fitbit, and she's taking better care of herself, but I don't think Dad is," she says softly later on, a little crestfallen. "But I'm glad he has it, and I'll just keep plugging along, trying to encourage him." No pressuring—such a wise young lady.

Sometimes KinKeeping is about respecting where people are and why they're there, even if we cannot help but nudge them toward better choices in tiny baby steps, at the rate they can accept and absorb.

Each of us always gets to choose
whether or not we receive a KinKeeper's offer.

Connecting at Rites of Passage

The receivers of the KinKeeping became KinKeepers themselves.

The couple lived on the west coast, but their wedding celebration would be in Oklahoma, since many of their friends and family live there. Some family members, musicians and other guests of honor would be coming from both coasts; some were sacrificing just to pay for plane tickets. Who would be able to help house them for the 4 nights they would spend in Tulsa?

To the KinKeepers in the couple's family and friends, it wasn't even a question. The bride's brother had a larger house and offered immediately to let seven guests stay with him. He and a friend shopped the local Farmer's Market for fresh veggies and herbs and made omelets for breakfast for the whole group. When a traveler's borrowed car broke down, another friend lent them his car, his only transportation, and he found ways to get around as needed.

More family members were housed with another brother and his wife. The groom's family housed guests and provided food and a huge barbecue event. Other traveler friends and musicians had rooms provided across the city by other wedding guests who lived locally. So many little get-togethers, so many lining up for bathroom/get-ready time, so many late-night conversations— KinKeeping at its finest, with a core "rite of passage"—a happy wedding!—at the center of all this connecting.

And the receivers of the KinKeeping became KinKeepers themselves, clearing away their mess, making up beds with fresh linens, leaving their borrowed rooms pristine and pretty, expressing their thanks and feeling the bonds of connection grow.

The web of back-and-forth giving and receiving becomes a strong lattice of support for KinKeepers who choose to intentionally nurture relationships and celebrate life events.

Friendships Across Age Brackets

I will always be thankful
for this gentle, feisty,
caring young woman who
was willing to become a
true friend to an older
coworker—and made my life
better.

I'm physically compromised. After an accident years ago where my friend's car was hit on the passenger side—where I was sitting—firemen had to remove me through the front windshield after using the "Jaws of Life" to make a way out of the car.

I had a concussion and was unconscious, my neck was hurt, and slivers of glass made their way up out of my skin for weeks afterward. Residual effects left me with vasovagal syncope, a condition that sometimes makes my already-low blood pressure fall lower still and my body then prepares to drop me to the floor to a horizontal position so that my brain and head get the oxygen they need. My youngest son, a chiropractic physician, directed me to chiropractic specialists who have made the difference for me— because of this care and Johnny's helpful tips on what to do when I feel something coming on, I'm able to conduct my life pretty much as I wish. But when I moved back to Oklahoma to be part of "the village" for my first granddaughter, I started having some trouble with those terrifying moments again, and more than once had to lie down on the floor at my new work place to avoid falling there, just to make it through my day.

Elizabeth, a young, bright, full-of-life co-worker, has fainted at inopportune times in her life, too—and so when she realizes what is happening with me, she takes care to KinKeep me. She always includes me in the conversations, she encourages me, tells me stories about her misfortunes, she generally befriends me and helps distract me to minimize my discomfort. She offers to drive me to appointments, brings me food, takes me under her wing.

I am not sure how I would have survived that first year back in Tulsa without this KinKeeper's inclusion and grace. After her beautiful wedding, she moved away, but we stay in touch.

Sharing Windfalls

Sharing windfalls
is a lovely way
to KinKeep

My friend is self-employed—also single and self-supporting. Her work-source has kind of dried up right when she finds herself needing to move out of her neighborhood because of dangerous activities close to her.

She has found another place, but costs are piling up: rental deposits, utility deposits, moving truck, on and on. It's almost overwhelming, and it's for-sure exhausting, with packing and cleaning, and all that needs to happen when you're changing locations. And she hasn't even had time to deal with the financial issues ahead of her with little work done to bring in paychecks.

And then a young friend connects with her and they go to grab lunch. The friend has just had a windfall financially—and she and her husband had looked at it incredulously—and immediately knew they were just the conduit. This money was for someone else; they would wait to see who it was that needed it.

Over lunch, the story comes out—my self-employed friend simply tells what has happened. She talks about how she is trusting that what she needs will be there when it's time to pay the next month's rent, to buy her groceries, to keep life going. The younger one instantly knows! She looks her in the eye and says, "I have your money. You are who this money is for." It's a sizeable chunk, too. Blown away, my friend cries with joy and appreciation. She feels KinKept.

She stayed in faith, and KinKeeping went into action;
she believes God moved in her universe through KinKeepers—
to help her get through this tough time.

Volunteer Tutoring

Volunteers in education
are priceless KinKeepers -
and change lives
on the daily,
while being changed,
themselves

Beth has a gift for tutoring. Or maybe it's a gift for loving. Either way, it's a beautiful thing to see in motion!

She works a fulltime job, has a partner and a teenager in her life, and yet makes time for years to tutor kids in reading twice a week. She came to it in mid-life, but once she found it, she jumped in with both feet. Spending time researching the Reading Partners program, getting tutoring tips, learning about her students' lives, helping them learn—she does it all, and oh my, she does this KinKeeping task well!

The kids she tutors make huge gains in their reading skills, comprehension skills, vocabulary ... and in their self-confidence. Beth digs in with them, gives help on the parts that make them stumble, then cheers them on when they grab the concept and gain new understanding.

For over two years, I sit near her at work, and I watch her bound into the office each time after she finishes her tutoring sessions. She is glowing and alight in her face, touched in her heart, and sometimes full of emotion that overflows as she exclaims over the cool things her student has accomplished that morning.

Each time her student benefits so much from the tutoring that he or she no longer needs it any longer, this KinKeeper is torn between joy for what that means to their lives—and sadness that she will no longer get to work with them in such a way.

She cares, deeply, and she put feet to her caring.

She's made a difference for these kids.

Modeling KinKeeping

Modeling KinKeeping and teaching children how to KinKeep is a wonderful way to pass it on, pay it forward, enrich children's lives, and show them the joy that can be found in both KinKeeping and being KinKept.

We're at the Splash Pad at the local park. It's our first time, it's roasting hot, and I've just picked up my granddaughter, Zoe, who is three years old.

I've brought her swimsuit and a towel, and I set her free to run and play in the water sprays. She immediately approaches the other kids playing there, saying, *"Hi! Let's play!"*

Some are interested, some are not—they just want to play by themselves. She figures this out and makes her little KinKeeping connections all on her own with the ones who do want to play. Soon she is chasing one right into the sprayer, and then the other kid is turning around, chasing her. They're connecting, laughing and having a good time.

Now another child comes, with her own plastic bucket and cup. Her mom knows this park and wisely brought toys to keep her daughter busy in the water. Zoe is instantly drawn to the bucket and the new child. *"Can you share me the bucket?"* she asks. The child ignores her and moves around her. One little sad face heads my way, and she asks, *"Do you have a bucket, Grandma?"* I had not thought about bringing any toys—so I help her find a little stick in the grass, and show her how to write lines with the wet stick on the sidewalk. But it's not enough. She's drawn to that bucket.

And here comes the KinKeeper! The other girl's mom is holding her hand, and together they bring the bucket to Zoe. *"You can have a turn now, if you want,"* she says. Zoe's little face shines as she accepts the bucket, takes her turn, fills and dumps it, throws it on herself, pours it out in a line, then hands it back.

I'm so grateful to the mother who wisely helped her child have the fun of graciously sharing with a stranger. The little one who shared claps and jumps up and down with joy. "My turn now!"

Sharing Day Care

Sharing day care among friends can be a fine way to KinKeep—everyone benefits!

Sharla and Krista are pretty much BFFs. One has four children, the other has five. Each has their youngest child still at home, so they've worked out a plan.

On Tuesdays, Sharla brings her little one to Krista's home for care, and Sharla gets the whole day to do all those things that are so much easier without small, precious ones around.

On Thursdays, Krista brings her youngest to Sharla's house for care—now she can have some lovely freedom. They're KinKeeping each other, as well as KinKeeping the kids.

And a side benefit is what happens between the little ones. With this regular contact, they now greet each other with hugs and smiles. They play together well for the most part, and they start KinKeeping each other, sharing toys, learning new things, becoming friends—just like their mothers.

And it spreads—older kids who get home from school while the littles are there become like big brothers and sisters to the visiting child, joining in the fun of KinKeeping.

Their worlds are all expanded; they are all more inclusive as they learn about diverse personalities, and work things out together.

What wonderful role modeling these kids get to experience!

This KinKeeping idea is a win for everyone!

Music Unites

My life would be
forever different,
expanded, because of
one band director's
willingness to invest
in KinKeeping me

Twice a week he met me early, before school. The old brown station wagon that served as our school bus in rural Clear Lake, South Dakota would arrive at the school 30 minutes before classes were to start. On Mondays and Wednesdays, I would jump out and run to the Band Room with my flute in hand, and Mr. Early would give me flute lessons—completely free. He gave his time to any child who wanted to learn an instrument.

I loved this KinKeeping time—the personal attention, the challenge to perform well, the training and teaching that was specific to me. All of it meant a lot, as I was one of seven children at home. In the world of music, I was my own person, yet part of something bigger; I understood now why certain sounds moved me, and rhythm compelled me.

Mr. Early's KinKeeping gave me access to music and I was determined to excel. So I practiced an hour a day, after farm chores in the afternoons or evenings, sitting on the edge of my parents' bed with my little music stand in front of me, playing my heart out.

Soon I was first chair in the flute section of the band, traveling on the big, yellow, "real" buses to football games and performing in concerts. My life would be forever different, expanded, because of one band director's willingness to invest in KinKeeping me—and many others, as well—with free music lessons. I still remember him with fondness.

Band directors, piano and instrument teachers, those who help anyone learn and enjoy music, all contribute immensely to our world. What a FUN way to KinKeep!

Please Call Again

*I think our perceptions
of KinKeeping can be felt
and enjoyed, even when
the "KinKeepers" don't
know they are providing
it for us!*

I must admit that my brother, Bill, is right - I can be pretty dense.

It takes me a while to "get" some things. I don't always think in straight, logical lines, and I take most things pretty literally.

Of course, over time, I've become able to laugh at myself and my rigid lines. I have worked to let go, and enjoy the sometimes wild paths that creativity can take me on when I let it—and I'm so much the better for that.

So when Bill and I reminisced recently, we both had a good laugh at an experience I remembered. I was about 8 years old, and we lived in an old farmhouse in South Dakota. We had no telephone yet, and whenever my parents needed to make a phone call, we would drive to town, go into the grocery store, ask to use the phone, and the owners would let us make our call.

The inside of the grocery store door had the words, *"Please Call Again,"* painted on it. As we would leave the store, I would see that sign, and get the warmest feeling in my heart. I felt KinKept.

Because when I read it, I thought it meant, *"Please, it's great! You can come and use our phone to call again and again, any time you need to. We're here for you!"* My little eight-year-old self loved that store and its owners because of that sign. I thought they were allies in our lives, people who were willing to share their telephone, and even invited us to do it again! I would hold my head high walking out of there, every time.

In my twenties, when I revisited that little town, and went to the store, the sign was still there—and even then, when I understood that *"Please call again"* really just meant, *"Please come again—and shop here"*, it still warmed my heart.

Sometimes KinKeeping happens ACCIDENTALLY!

Family Support

Those who KinKeep by kindly sharing their lives with others may nurture new, innovative growth in them—as well as enrich their own lives by having this other person in their midst.

My dad's brother, Jim, was my favorite uncle, as he and Aunt Gladys definitely took a shine to us kids. Uncle Jim worked building roads in Minnesota, and he would pull his tiny little travel trailer along with him when working more than an hour away from his home in Porter. Three times, he and my dad found ways to connect to transfer me to stay with them for a week in the summer—and so I got to spend time in a different world.

This was back in 1957. I would stay with Aunt Gladys during the days in some little tiny town's parking spot for trailers. She would take walks with me, we would bake and cook together, and I would have time to read and think and talk with her, even play spelling games, which I loved. Then Uncle Jim would finish his shift, come back to the trailer all grimy and hot, get cleaned up—and we'd drive to some lake or park area and eat our supper together—and talk some more. For once, I would be the ONLY kid—and have a chance to have all the attention! I would be spoiled and doted on, fussed over. I'd see things and places I had never seen, watch how other families did things, and feel like I was special.

Any time one child in a family spends time with a different family or in a different situation, the dynamic is changed, their world gets bigger, their perspective changes. Those who KinKeep by kindly sharing their lives with others may nurture new, innovative growth in them—as well as enrich their own lives.

And for those left at home, the dynamic changes, too—when I later became mother to four children, and a friend would say, *"Well, does it even help if I just take one of the kids for a few hours or a day or two?"* I would instantly say, *"Oh, yes! That changes things up around here, and the kids relate differently to each other. And we get to hear from the ones who don't usually speak up. It's a tremendous gift to have a chance to tweak the family structure for even a couple of hours."*

Expanding others' worlds is one helpful aspect of KinKeeping.

KinKeeping Your Self

I began
KinKeeping myself
long before
I knew the word
for it.

I became my own
cheerleader.

In an exercise program called Callanetics, I unwisely bounced
on an already stretched-out muscle in my leg. That poor muscle
ruptured with a loud, suction-y kind of noise, heard by everyone
in the room. I crumpled, in terrible pain.

My recovery was long and humbling. Doctors' instructions were to
immobilize my leg, only move around as I had to in order to keep
life going. It was miserable, being in pain, spending my days in a
chair trying to keep my family's life going. I could not be productive
any longer! Having long based my sense of self-worth on what I was
able to produce, or accomplish, this was very difficult for me.

One day, home alone, I spent 90 minutes just getting myself to the
bathtub, taking a bath, getting dressed, and finally, sitting down on
the edge of my bed, across from my dresser mirror. I looked defeated,
bedraggled. I started talking to my self in the mirror.

*"That was a marathon. I am exhausted, just from getting ready for
the day. I feel like I deserve some kind of prize, just for getting dressed
today! How come there's no one who realizes what this is costing me?
How come no one is applauding me for all the courage it's taking just to
keep going on? I don't get to do any work that contributes to life for any
of us lately, all I can do is try to get well. No one notices! Nobody cares!
I need a best friend here with me to hold me up and encourage me."*

Wah, wah, wah. I had a real pity party. Still sitting there, because I
literally was too tired to move. As I sat there, my crying stopped as
the thought occurred to me, and I said it out loud: *"I have to be my
own best friend. I have to be my own cheerleader. No one else could
possibly KNOW what it's like to be me. And I'm going to do it. I'm going
to get through this! I am enough, I have value, whether or not I can
do anything at all."* I knew the truth as soon as it came out of my
mouth. I sat up straighter, I felt different.

I could nurture and KinKeep my own self! And I did.

115

KinKeeping Grandkids

Sometimes, KinKeepers must make hard choices to triage KinKeeping activities, devoting their energy and resources to attending first to those most vulnerable, those who cannot help themselves

What in the world? Mary hung up the phone. All her energy was gone, all the way down to her toes.

Her only son's one call from jail had just been used up, to call her. Possession of drugs with intent to sell, although he said the stash under the driver's seat was not his, but instead belonged to the guy he was giving a ride home to.

Tears sprang to her eyes as she leaned forward and bowed her head. *"Help me, God,"* she cried. *"My son, my son—please let him not be sellling drugs again! I can't go through that one more time.*

I cannot bail him out this time—the best way to KinKeep him now is to just be in his corner, caring, loving, encouraging him to make good choices and cheering him on as HE digs his own way through and out of this.

No ... I must save my strength to be there for my granddaughter; she's the innocent victim of his actions."

Sometimes, KinKeepers must make hard choices to *triage* KinKeeping activities, devoting their energy and resources to attending first to those most vulnerable, those who cannot help themselves.

And so Grandma Mary takes in a tender two-year-old,
rearranges her entire life around daycare and diapers,
and puts her dreams of retirement on hold while
Brittney grows up.

Traditions Continue

I shake my head.
Paperchains —
the circle continues.

Onward with KinKeeping!

That big astonished smile that only a 2-year-old can do justice to! I watch her turn her charm on her 5-year-old friend, and I remember fondly their mothers at those ages. Time stands still as the new generation sits at the kitchen table, construction paper everywhere, with those tiny, very-wet, folded brown paper towels laid out for them to use. We've even gotten the popsicle sticks and a jar of that great school paste.

Just like what we used when we were that age!

I have already cut some paper strips, but the 5-year-old wants to cut his own. And he does. Just fine. They're having their own messy adventure, gluing and pasting, and making paperchains.

Needs no help from a grandma—except to look over their shoulder, smile a lot, and cheer them on.

Today they are making the next generation of paperchains ... and growing closer together through this shared experience.

I smile to see the next generation of Kin.

KinKept by SomeOne/SomeThing Bigger Than Ourselves

Always believing
there is something
more than this plane
of living,
I was KinKept
first
by that reassurance

I know you are there, God, Higher Power, Universe, angels ...

I see now that perhaps you are not exactly as I was taught, and certainly not exactly as anyone else claims you to be.

But oh, I know YOU are there, embedding moral principles throughout my world.

I am held in your hands. I am connected to you.

I am valued by you.

And every other person on this earth is also valued by you.

Each one is just as important as I am.

We need each other—as together we learn about life!
Created with a need to belong, to be part of the larger,our lives become rich as we respect, value, and nurture the living people and things in our world.

God, by any name, and in any language
held holy in the heart,

You are the original KINKEEPER who deeply desires connection
And who makes it happen—

Thank you that I am indeed KinKept by you

And that I am ever aware of the KinKeepers around me

And continually nudged to follow your example
to KinKeep.

Recognizing Everyone's Value

We are better connected
to each other and to
life, because of knowing
Rosemond, because one
person took time to see and
hear us, KinKeeping us
as she acknowledges our
contribution to the world

Rosemond values people. She sees each one—no one is beneath her. She looks people in the eye, she pays attention to names, she addresses everyone with a profound respect, she practices the Golden Rule, and ... she KinKeeps as a way of life. It is intrinsic in her to care about and establish a connection with each person in her path.

We teach others how to treat us, by how we treat them and by what treatment we expect from them—and Rosemond has taught us to treat her well. She carries "class" around with her like a cloud of sweet-smelling perfume, and wafts it upon us by her very presence. Her regal bearing is best accentuated when she's in her colorful native Ghanaian turban, but even in American dress, she is always regal.

She walks into our area at work with a heartfelt note of gratitude, her biggest smile, and homemade treats for us all. She wants to thank us for administrative services rendered.

To a person, we feel honored to know her, and, as we gather to receive from her hand, the brownies she has prepared become almost an element of communion.

After she leaves, we hover near the treats. Talk is hushed and respectful. Often unnoticed in the tasks we do, we have been recognized, valued, honored. It is nearly a holy moment—and we all feel it.

We are better connected to each other and to life, because of knowing Rosemond, because one person took time to see and hear us, and acknowledge our contribution to their world.

I hope you have enjoyed these little KinKeeping stories ... and I hope they've provoked some thought for you. They are just the tiniest fraction of the stories I hold in my heart, my mind, my memory. These are a few from my world, from my frame of reference, from my experience, or those I witnessed as a bystander.

They've warmed my heart for such a long time—and I'm so glad to share them!

But I know they are such a small sliver of the KinKeeping stories in our world! Your experience with your family, with your aunties and uncles, with your grandparents—oh, these stories have much to teach us all! And how your bowling group from high school days still gets together—who makes that happen? What about the Wednesday night volleyball games with food and drink afterwards that you've been part of long years? How does any of that keep on happening, and what does it mean in your life?

And what precious gems of KinKeeping ideas lie in cultures much different from my Minnesota memories? What are the foods whose very smells wrap you with love and take you back to your ethnic heritage? What traditions were passed down to you in your family of origin, in your in-laws' families, in the family-groups you have created for yourself of the people on the earth that you feel like really know and accept you and love you, your family created by choice? Where do you belong—and who helped provide that feeling for you?

****

Who snuggles you in close and nurtures you when times are hard? Who really "sees" you and "hears" you? Who actually "gets" you? Who always remembers that you exist?

These are the conversations I hope our world can share more and more of in the future. *KinKept: Intentionally Nurturing Connections* is meant to be just the first little tiny entry in a huge array of story-sharing. My hope is that you're inspired even just a little bit by one of these tellings—and it makes you think of something you would like to do to build stronger connections between you and someone. you care about. Or that it makes you think of a special thing that made you feel KinKept.

I know that every single KinKeeping event that occurred for me was a real privilege—something I did nothing to deserve—and I'm thankful for every time I was KinKept or saw KinKeeping happen.

However, I think we are all aware that not everyone gets excited hearing about KinKeeping. For some among us, there wasn't much KinKeeping happening—and they become sad just thinking about that. I'm so sorry if that's true for you. I hope that looking back through the lens of seeking out the KinKeepers in your world will reveal someone, something that acted on your life in a KinKeeping manner. Something that kept you alive, kept you hoping, kept you attached to life itself. Something you would like to celebrate and pass on.

Clearly, everyone's KinKeeping stories will be very different. The background of a simple rural Midwestern farm in the 1950s and 1960s is obviously unique to a small number of people. It's real for me—and yours is real for you.

Your own background and culture will mean your KinKeeping stories will have your own flavor, your own treasured memories. They will be peopled with your own characters, hardships, joys of connecting. AND your own innovative or timeworn KinKeeping activities that worked to help keep you and yours connected around that warm fire of love and caring. I yearn for us all to learn new ideas of connecting activities from each other!

And I'm hoping maybe you can warm yourself at the fire of other people's stories and get inspired to **create** some KinKeeping for your own Crew. If you care about someone, and hope to feel connected to them, perhaps you will try a little reaching out to them. See what happens. Think of yourself as a KinKeeper; see what happens to the thoughts in your mind, and the actions you start to take—thoughts and actions of connecting to the world around you. Strengthening connections for others and yourself through your KinKeeping offers and actions can be a very lovely adventure!

****

Spread the Word About KinKeeping

Plans are in place for new editions of little KinKeeping books, stories, even lessons for those who may not have had much modeling of KinKeeping done for them, in the way that I was privileged to have. A primer of more ideas, thoughts and basic principles for KinKeeping will be the next KinBook to emerge in the KinBook Collection. Watch for it out soon!

You can check out my website, **www.kinkeeping.com** to see what new projects, ideas, information, and thoughts to ponder are listed at any given time. I hope to stir up conversations, provoke thought, and increase appreciation in our world for **all you wonderful KinKeepers!** AND I hope we can all learn from each other—and in the process, increase our feeling of being connected to each other and to our world.

Best of all, I hope you'll share with me a story of a KinKeeping thought or practice you'd like the world to learn from. You'll find a place to share that story on www.kinkeeping.com—perhaps it will find a way into one of the next KinKeeping books!

About the Author

Judy Keefe has always loved words, both reading and writing them. She's won awards for her poetry, been published in magazines and op-ed pieces, and is always looking to inspire and encourage others to use their gifts and talents.

Judy is the author of *First Person Singular, Monologues in a Poetic Mode*, published by Lillenas Publishing House, Kansas City, MO.

Following a varied career encompassing work as an administrative assistant, executive assistant, mental health family skills practitioner, juvenile probation officer, and writer/ Instructional Designer, Judy moved into an encore career working to provoke thought and encourage connections on the planet.

She is also the owner of KinKopy Writing Services, www.kinkopy. com.

For more information on KinKeeping and on being KINKEPT, please refer to www.kinkeeping.com